Published in 2000 by Creative Education
123 South Broad Street, Mankato, Minnesota 56001
Creative Education is an imprint of The Creative Company

Designed by Stephanie Blumenthal
Production Design by Beowulf Ltd.

Photographs by Derek Fell

Library of Congress Cataloging-in-Publication Data

Fell, Derek
Orchids / by Derek Fell
Includes glossary and index
Summary: Describes the history of orchids, various types of this exotic
flower, and how they are cultivated
ISBN 1-58341-003-1
1. Orchids—Juvenile literature. [1. Orchids.] I. Title. II. Series:
Let's Investigate (Mankato, Minn.)
QK495.064F42   1999
584'.4—dc21   99-11607

First edition

2 4 6 8 9 7 5 3 1

ORCHIDS

DEREK FELL

Creative Education

ORCHID
COLLECTION

Durban Botanical Gardens, South Africa, features the largest orchid collection in the world, composed of thousands of species and hybrids in rock gardens and pools.

4

ORCHID
S H O W

Longwood Gardens, Pennsylvania, provides a spectacular indoor orchid display every February, composed of hundreds of cymbidium *orchids grown in pots.*

Cymbidium orchids

Orchids are the largest plant family on Earth, with an estimated 25,000 species, or kinds, growing in a wide range of climates and habitats from Alaska to the tropics. Though the most beautiful kinds are tropical, growing outdoors in a humid, frost-free **environment**, many of these can be raised indoors as house plants. Many are the main attraction of arboretums. These glass-enclosed houses showcase a variety of plants and flowers from all around the world.

ORCHID
SOCIETY

The American Orchid Society has more than 30,000 members; it is the largest plant society in North America.

ORCHID
FACT

Orchids grow from sea level to an altitude of 14,000 feet (4,267 m), from the Arctic Circle to the Sub-Antarctic.

Each orchid species has distinct colors and markings

ORCHIDS AS PLANTS

There are a lot of reasons why orchids are so fascinating to study. Many orchid collectors say the biggest attraction is their near-human characteristics, with personalities and "faces" formed by their distinctive flower shape, exotic colors, and bizarre petal markings. Indeed, orchids are skillful **mimics**. In order to attract insect **pollinators**, some orchid flowers imitate female moths and bees. When insects attempt to mate with the plant, they unwittingly engage in an act of cross-**pollination** that allows the orchid to set seed for a new generation.

Orchid throats resemble insects

Basically, an orchid flower consists of an arrangement of six petals (three are actually sepals—modified leaves that look like petals); the lower petal is often frilly and large and known as a "lip." There is a nose-like extension at the center of each flower, called a column, with a sticky head that aids in the transfer of **pollen**. No other flower family features this column. Some orchid flowers—such as *cattleyas*—are large and flamboyant, but others can be tiny and inconspicuous. The color range is extensive, and many orchids are bi-colored (having two colors) and tri-colored (having three).

ORCHID

In a world of an estimated 250,000 flowering plant species, more than one in ten is an orchid.

ORCHID

W I L D

The marsh orchid is a hardy perennial, growing wild in marshy areas throughout southwestern Europe, but it is the easiest orchid to grow in northern home gardens.

Lady's slippers growing in the wild (right) and planted in a hanging basket (opposite)

In the wild, orchids can be terrestrial (meaning they grow on the ground) or epiphytic (meaning they grow on other plants—usually in the crotches of trees). There is even an Australian variety that is subterranean—growing and flowering completely underground.

Another unusual fact about orchids is that many varieties depend on soil fungi called *Mycorrhiza*. The fungi and these orchids have a symbiotic relationship, meaning they depend on each other to survive.

ORCHID HISTORY

The ancient Chinese civilizations were the first to collect orchid plants from the wild and use them to beautify their homes and gardens. Their orchids were mostly tree-dwelling types, transferred to hanging baskets and displayed outdoors in a window or in the shade of a tree, especially in **monasteries**.

9

ORCHID
COLOR

The jewel orchid has chocolate colored leaves striped with orange veins.

Above, gold-lace orchid
Right, wild orchids can bloom profusely

Spanish **conquistadors** returned from South and Central America in 1510 with the vanilla orchid, the first exotic orchid to reach Europe from the tropics. The vanilla orchid is a vining plant that produces green flowers and a long brown bean-shaped pod. This pod is the source of vanilla flavoring—the most popular ice cream flavor in the world.

Not until the early 1800s—when plant explorers to South and Central America brought back information about growing conditions—did Europeans take an active interest in orchid culture. This new understanding of growing orchids in Victorian England coincided with two important inventions: greenhouses and the Wardian case. Greenhouses are glass structures that can be heated year-round to protect plants from frost. A Wardian case was a portable glass container that allowed orchids to be carried safely across long distances by ship.

ORCHIDS
INDOORS

*A good way to grow orchids indoors is in hanging baskets, especially in a sunny **conservatory**.*

Left, orchid blossoms look delicate but last a long time Above, fried-egg orchid

ORCHID

Many orchids must be at least four years old in order to flower, and sometimes they must be as old as twelve.

Right, dancing lady orchids
Below, orchid blossoms make beautiful bouquets or corsages

12

After the Austrian monk, Gregor Mendel, published his studies of **genetics** in 1866, planters learned how to cross different species of orchids to create **hybrids**, generating shapes and color combinations never seen before.

The easiest orchids to grow for decorative value indoors are *cattleyas* (florist orchids), *paphiopedilums* (slipper orchids), *phalaenopsis* (moth orchids), *miltonias* (pansy orchids), and *cymbidiums* (mountain orchids). They are all tender and require frost protection.

ORCHID
O D O R S

*Some orchids—like the florist orchid—are pleasantly fragrant to attract birds and bats for pollination. Other orchids can smell like rotting meat to attract **carrion** flies.*

13

Rock garden filled with orchids

ORCHID

When the seed capsule of an orchid is ripe, it bursts open and the seeds are distributed by the wind. Very few of the seeds grow, however, since orchid seeds need a special fungus to survive.

14

Right, Elizabeth Straus orchid Opposite, close view of a lady's slipper throat

The florist orchids (*cattleyas*) are native to the **rain forests** of Central and South America, where they grow high in the tree canopy attached to tree limbs. They are highly fragrant and popular among florists for wedding **corsages** and as flowering gift plants.

ORCHID

The Chinese fairy orchid will tolerate mild frosts, allowing it to be grown outdoors in the Western and Gulf states.

16

Center, wild lady's slippers
Below, many orchids grow hanging in groups or clusters

Slipper orchids (*paphiopedilums*) are named for their lower petals which are fused to form a shoe shape. They are native to countries in Asia, growing mostly on the ground in shady locations.

oth orchids (*phalaenopsis*) are mostly white. They are clustered so many to a stem that they look like a flock of moths or butter-flies in flight. They are native to Malaysia. Growing in the forest close to streams, pools, and lagoons, they arch their flowers over the water.

ORCHID
SIZE

Some florist orchids have flowers as large as dinner plates—the smallest orchid flowers are no bigger than a flea.

Many orchids resemble lilies

ORCHID
COLORS

The most highly desirable color among orchid collectors is blue, but green, brown, and nearly black are also highly prized.

Miltonias are called pansy orchids because their flowers are shaped like a pansy. Discovered in Brazil, they attract moths as pollinators, and the center of each flower mimics a female moth in flight, encouraging male moths to land on the flower for pollination.

Right, pansey orchid
Above, moth orchid

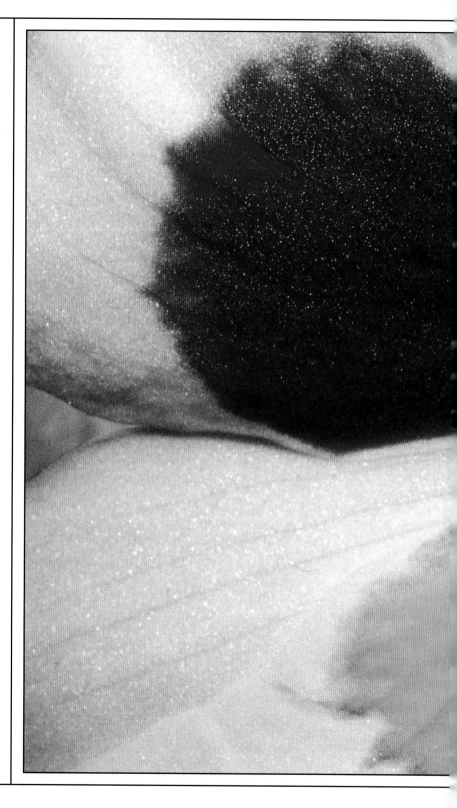

ORCHID
DISPLAY

In frost-free areas it is possible to grow orchids outdoors. The best way to display them is growing among rocks in the shade of trees or shrubs, especially surrounding a pool to provide the humidity they enjoy.

Two varieties of cybidiums are the Finetta G (right) and the Sussex orchid (above)

Cymbidiums are from India. They are found mostly in the foothills of the Himalaya Mountains. The large star-shaped flowers are clustered on long arching stems that last a long time when cut and placed in water.

ORCHIDS IN THE WILD

North America has 150 species of wild orchids, the most interesting of which is the pink ladyslipper. It grows mostly in woodland clearings in the eastern part of North America from Georgia to Canada. Although it is hardy, it is a favorite food of deer, so the natural populations have been diminishing at an alarming rate. Some specialist wildflower nurseries offer plants to grow in home gardens, but trying to transplant them to your own property is unreliable.

ORCHID
F A C T

*Tree-growing orchids have fat pseudobulbs (also called rhizomes) to store moisture for long periods of drought. They also have **aerial roots** capable of extracting moisture from the atmosphere.*

Orchids grow well in the shade of trees

ORCHID
TRAVEL

Microscopic orchid seeds can be carried great distances from their place of origin, even hidden in the feathers of birds.

ORCHID
FACT

*Though orchids such as dendrobiums are epiphytic (living in trees), they are not **parasites** and cause no harm to the tree.*

Right, "The Giant" Opposite, grand monarch orchid

ORCHID NURSERIES

As the public interest in orchids has increased, orchid nurseries have been established to meet the demand. They are especially popular as gifts on Easter and Mother's Day. Cut orchid stems are also popular year-round as corsages at prom dances and bouquets at weddings. Some nurseries in Florida and California also produce mail-order catalogs for orchid collectors.

ORCHID

After pollination, orchids produce seed pods called capsules; a single capsule can contain up to five million seeds as small as dust.

ORCHID

RELATIVE

The nearest plant relative to the orchid is the iris.

Orchid pool

To operate a successful orchid nursery, it is necessary to have a warm greenhouse with high **humidity** and good air circulation. Orchids are susceptible to a number of plant diseases, so hygiene is extremely important.

Traditionally, raising orchids was expensive, involving seed starting (a slow process) and dividing up plants that produced *rhizomes*—a swollen root that can be removed to create a new plant.

25

Colorific orchid

Since 1960, orchid nurseries have changed over to a system called *meristem* culture. This allows a large number of plants to be grown from a small piece of the parent plant. A section of living tissue—usually from the rhizome—is placed in a test tube on top of special **nutrients** and encouraged to sprout in a laboratory. Once the sprouting has occurred and the juvenile plant is large enough to handle, it is then transplanted to a pot and grown in the nursery to flower. This process has greatly reduced the cost of raising orchids since it is now possible to produce thousands of plants from a single parent.

ORCHID

MEADOW

The buttonhole orchid is used by people in Hawaii to create wildflower meadows around their homes.

Right, orchids in large patio pots Above, orchids in small pots

GROWING ORCHIDS AT HOME

Though orchids have a reputation for being difficult to grow indoors, certain kinds are relatively easy as house plants. They can be raised in a sun room or on a windowsill (but avoid direct sunlight). In areas with mild winters, such as Florida and southern California, orchids can be grown outdoors year-round.

The best orchids to start with are the florist orchids (or *cattleyas*)—especially a group of hybrids known as *Lailio-cattleyas*. These plants do not require such high temperatures or high humidity as other orchids, and they are easily grown in a flower pot. *Pleione* orchids (or Chinese fairy orchids), which look like miniature *cattleyas*, are also good to start in flower pots. In southern states and California they will spend winter outdoors in shady locations. Like most other orchids, they like a soil that drains well, especially a mix of peat, pine bark, and **sphagnum moss**.

ORCHID
POLLEN

The pollen of orchids is not exposed in a ring of yellow **stamens** *like other plants. It is encased in a pair of small sticky pouches that must be carried from flower to flower by insects or bats.*

27

Orchids are stunning

Looking at the special soil that orchids need can make for a challenging study, or even a science fair project. Experiments with soil and nutrient content on different kinds of plants can reveal valuable information about how these plants use food. Experiments with light, temperature, humidity levels, and even the use of various fertilizers can reveal how plants turn light, water, and soil nutrients into the energy that makes them grow.

ORCHID
PINK

*Terrestrial orchids—
such as the pink
ladyslipper—are
hardy plants, but
they require a special
soil fungus around
their roots to survive.*

ORCHID
DANCERS

*The flowers of the
dancing lady orchid
look like dancing
ladies with out-
stretched arms,
small waists, and
flared skirts.*

**Cymbidiums (center
and next page)
Page 31, close view
of Vesuvius orchid**

Most botanical gardens have orchid displays where you can learn about the particular varieties that appeal to you. Orchid shows organized by chapters of the North American Orchid Society are also worth visiting for information about growing orchids. These fascinating and beautiful plants are truly gems of the flower world. With new varieties created every year, they will continue to be enjoyed by orchid collectors and flower-lovers alike.

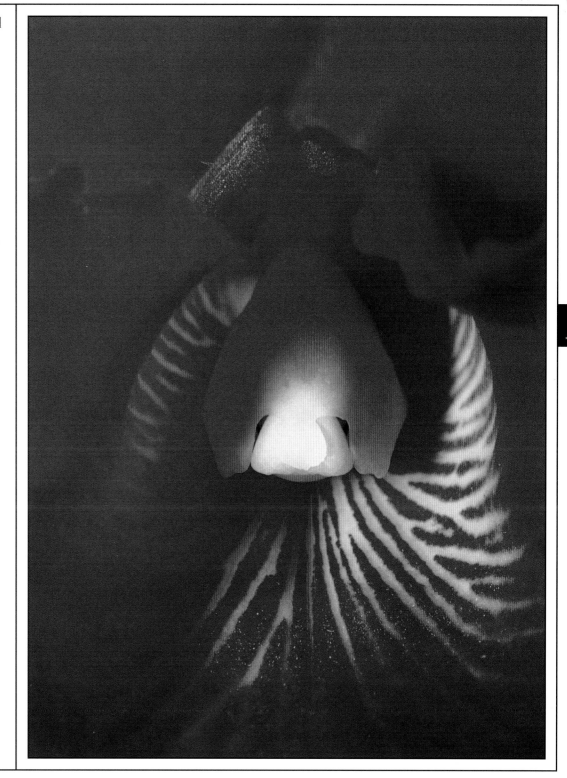

Glossary

Aerial roots draw nutrients and moisture from the air, as opposed to roots that draw them from the soil.

Carrion is dead and decaying meat.

The Spanish **conquistadors** were soldier-explorers seeking conquest of newly discovered territory.

A sun-room or glasshouse for decorative plants is a **conservatory**.

Corsages are small floral arrangements worn by women for special occasions.

The word **environment** refers to a plant's natural surroundings.

Genetics is the scientific study of characteristics that are passed on from parents to their young.

Humidity is moisture-filled air.

Hybrids are created when scientists cross two plant or animal species that do not normally mate.

Mimics imitate the look or sound of a person or thing.

Monks live and practice their religion in **monasteries**.

Plants need **nutrients** (food) in order to survive.

Parasites are plants or animals that live on another living being, called the "host." Eventually, the parasites can completely destroy the host.

Pollen are tiny dust-like particles that fertilize plants; the transfer of pollen to fertilize plants is called pollination.

Pollination is the transfer of pollen grains between plants. This results in fruit formation and seed production. **Pollinators** are agents (bees, bats, even the wind) that cause the transfer of pollen.

Rain forests are tropical jungles that have excessive amounts of moisture, encouraging the trees to grow very tall, and sheltering a great diversity of plant and animal life.

Sphagnum moss is a cushion-shaped moss that can be dried to create a suitable potting mixture for many orchids.

The male reproductive organs of flowering plants—the part that produces pollen—is called the **stamens**.

Index